The Gay Slayer

The Life of Serial Killer Colin Ireland

ABSOLUTE CRIME

By Fergus Mason

Absolute Crime Books

www.absolutecrime.com

© 2014. All Rights Reserved.

Cover Image © Ekler - Fotolia.com

Table of Contents

ABOUT US **3**
INTRODUCTION **4**
    March 8 11
CHAPTER 1 .... **19**
CHAPTER 2 .... **26**
    May 28 31
CHAPTER 3 .... **37**
CHAPTER 4 .... **47**
    June 4 50
CHAPTER 5 .... **62**
CHAPTER 6 .... **67**
    June 7 70
CHAPTER 7 .... **80**
CHAPTER 8 .... **84**
    June 12 89
CHAPTER 9 .... **94**
CHAPTER 10 .... **100**
CONCLUSION **104**

About Us

Absolute Crime publishes only the best true crime literature. Our focus is on the crimes that you've probably never heard of, but you are fascinated to read more about. With each engaging and gripping story, we try to let readers relive moments in history that some people have tried to forget.

Remember, our books are not meant for the faint at heart. We don't hold back — if a crime is bloody, we let the words splatter across the page so you can experience the crime in the most horrifying way!

If you enjoy this book, please visit our homepage to see other books we offer; if you have any feedback, we'd love to hear from you!

Introduction

Apart from complaining about the weather few things are as British as a traditional neighborhood pub. The image of a friendly bar where everyone knows everyone else is a common feature in TV and movies, and it's pretty closely based on reality. Everything changes though, and now when the British aren't discussing the rain they'll often talk about how there aren't enough proper pubs left these days. It's easy to see what they mean. Too many old-style locals have been taken over by national chains and remodeled into soulless identikit franchises. Interiors that have evolved over decades or even centuries have been ripped out and replaced with Ikea-style modern furniture or – even worse – fake memorabilia. Changing demographics, falling alcohol consumption and the 2007 smoking ban have driven thousands of pubs into bankruptcy and forced thousands more to rely more on food sales. That's good if you're looking for a reasonably priced place to take the family for dinner. It's not always so great if you want somewhere to drink and relax with friends.

The Pembroke Inn, a remodeled bar in London's Earl's Court district, is a typical modern gastropub. Located in a three-story brick building, the exterior hasn't changed much since it opened in 1866. It's all brown marble cladding and dark green cement moldings, small-paned windows and flowers in hanging baskets. It sits on a T-junction, and there are three entrances – one each on Coleherne Road and Old Brompton Road, and the main one right on the corner itself. Since it was refurbished by a major pub chain the old signs have been replaced by a minimalist logo of a simple large P, and a few small tables on the sidewalk outside give it a European café feeling when the weather's good. Inside, half of the old horseshoe-shaped bar is now dedicated to food. The Pembroke is trying hard to rise above the standard microwaved pub meals and each plate that comes from the kitchen is artfully arranged and garnished. The menu is trendy-cosmopolitan – halloumi and quinoa, braised rabbit ragu over pappardelle, vegetarian Indian platter for two – and the bar snack list includes Cretan olives and chickpea fritters. Draft and bottled beers come from around Europe, and there's Prosecco on tap. Even at 6:00pm on a Thursday it's busy. The crowd is young, groups of friends laughing on the big chesterfield sofas and a lot of couples. The main bar is bright and airy, and there's also a music bar upstairs and a beer garden out back.

It wasn't always like this. The Pembroke Inn was once The Coleherne, a Victorian working mens' pub that started attracting actors from nearby theaters sometime in the 1930s. By the 50s it had become a gay bar and over the next two decades it slowly morphed into the center of London's leather and bondage scene. It's that period in the pub's long history I've gone there to learn about.

The Pembroke is busy enough that I have to take care as I weave my way to the door clutching two pints of Bitburger, but I make it past the knot of smokers outside the door and sit down at one of the tables. Sitting opposite is a fit-looking man in his early 60s, dressed smart but casual and quietly respectable. He wasn't always like this either. He first visited The Coleherne nearly four decades ago, at the height of its notoriety, and was a regular visitor through to the mid-1990s. Today he insists on sitting outside, at this wobbly table. That's not because of loyalty to its old identity or to avoid painful memories; it's because he's smoking a steady chain of Gauloises and doesn't want to keep interrupting to stand outside the door. Sitting outside is okay though. It's cloudy this evening, but mild and dry.

"It wouldn't have mattered, then," he says. "The place was a blue fog. Smelled like an ashtray of course." There are no ashtrays on the tables today, and my companion scowls distastefully every time he flicks a butt into the street. "God, it was rough. Then again that was the attraction. The gay scene around the West End was fucking awful, you know," he affects an effeminate lisp, "*dreadfully* camp, dahling. All mincing old queens and skinny little fairies sipping Babycham. This place was different."

It certainly was. The Coleherne was an international mecca for the leather crowd and it had an almost cultivated air of seediness. The windows that now flood the place with daylight were mostly covered with flyers advertising bands or nightclubs (for a while they were even blacked out with paint) and the interior was dim, loud, smoky and vaguely menacing. Its ethos had been shaped in the 60s and 70s, when openly gay couples still weren't welcome – and sometimes weren't safe – in mainstream pubs, and even in the 1990s it maintained a defiant, almost aggressive outrageousness. Gay celebrities, many of them still in the closet, were regular visitors; the tabloid press didn't venture into The Coleherne's murky depths, so it was a place they could relax and be themselves. Comedian Kenny Everett was well known there, as were *Psycho* star Anthony Perkins and dancer Rudolf Nureyev. Queen front man Freddie Mercury, at the height of his fame, used to slip gratefully into the anonymity of The Coleherne. Its fame even spread to gay capital San Francisco, when author Armistead Maupin mentioned it in his novel *Babycakes*.

"Basically it was the opposite of a celebrity nightspot," he says. "Somewhere like Stringfellows, you go there to be seen. This was a place you came to hide. Or enjoy a bit of rough, of course. Couples diving into the broom cupboard for a quickie, the toilets ankle deep in piss… not classy."

I ask about the secret code that regulars used to identify their sexual preferences – it's a key part of the story I'm interested in. The Coleherne's clientele included many with specialized tastes, some of which would be awkward to ask a stranger about.

"Oh, the handkerchiefs? Yes, some people did that. Bit of an affectation really." He suddenly realizes there's an ashtray bolted to the wall a foot behind him, and sheepishly drops his latest butt into it. "Probably somebody brought the idea back from San Francisco and it caught on. Just imagine, all those pasty-faced Englishmen going for the California look." Two young men, obviously gay, walk out of the Pembroke and look around for a cab. He points them out with a nod. "They'd have hated the place back then. Far too grotty for them." He plucks another cigarette from the pack. "Personally I loved it. There was just this amazing buzz of rebelliousness, of not giving a shit what people thought." He picks up his lighter then suddenly frowns, toying with it for a moment. "And danger, of course. Yes, there was always a hint of danger in the air."

March 8

Old Brompton Road, Earl's Court, London

Peter Walker paid off the cab on Old Brompton Road, half a block from his destination. He loitered for a few moments while the driver U-turned and drove off towards Kensington, then rummaged in the pocket of his leather jacket and pulled out a small wad of cloth. Unfolded, it was a cheerfully embroidered black handkerchief. As he walked the fifty yards to the corner of Old Brompton and Colehern he carefully tucked a corner of it into the back pocket of his jeans. Hanging down over his right buttock, the black hanky indicated that he'd like to be the submissive partner in a sadomasochistic bondage game.

After the cool March night walking in the door of The Coleherne was an assault on the senses. It was a Monday and most people were taking it easy after the weekend, but not here. The bar was crowded and the air thick with cigarette smoke. Right Said Fred's "I'm Too Sexy" blasted from the speakers, half-drowning the chaotic babble of voices and laughter. Pushing his way through the throng, Walker found himself a place at the bar and started trying to catch the barman's eye. Even as he waited to be served he was already scanning the crowd, checking out handkerchiefs where they were on display. He was looking for a black hanky in the left back pocket – the sign of a dominant sadist. If he saw one he'd approach the wearer; otherwise he'd wait for someone to come on to him.

Walker, a 45-year-old choreographer and director who worked in the West End theater business, had recently been diagnosed as HIV positive. On the plus side, he'd been hired as assistant director on *City of Angels*, a film noir-inspired musical that had just finished a successful run on Broadway and was due to open later that month at the Prince of Wales Theatre. His diagnosis had left him depressed, though, and he'd been feeling lonely and isolated for the last few months.[i] His beloved dogs gave him some company, but he hated returning to an empty apartment. To fill the void he'd started hanging out at The Coleherne. The men he met there would never play a major part in his life but with the shadow of HIV hanging over him he wasn't all that worried about the future.

Sipping his beer slowly, not rushing it, Walker waited for something to happen. There were several men he knew scattered around the bar. Mentally he considered each of them, but ruled them out one by one. There was no hurry – he had hours before closing time. As time passed though, he found his gaze turning more and more often to a man sitting alone at one of the small tables. Walker had never seen him in here before, and he was intrigued.

Curious now, Walker studied the man. He was tall and muscular, dressed casually – no ostentatious leather, just jeans and a T-shirt – and seemed faintly out of place. Next time he visited the restroom he made a point of detouring behind the man on his way back, hoping to check out his back pockets for a clue. Yes! There it was – a black handkerchief. And it was on the left; the stranger was dominant. That was just what Walker was looking for. As a sub he usually waited for others to approach him. This time, he decided, he was going to take the initiative.

With a fresh beer in his hand Walker drifted casually over to the stranger's table and asked if he could sit down.

The big man looked up at Walker. Just for a moment his face seemed to cloud with apprehension, then it cleared as if a decision had been made. Later he would tell police, "I thought to myself if I'm approached, something will happen. If I'm not… It would have been quite likely I would have gone on my way and nothing would have happened."[ii] Now the die was cast; something was going to happen.

The two quickly fell into a conversation. Walker was just looking for a casual fling, so he didn't probe too deeply into the other man's background or motivations. Instead, he discreetly sounded him out to see if he would be interested in spending the night together. It gradually became obvious that he would. The stranger – his name was Colin, he said – seemed slightly awkward, but he hinted that he'd be keen to play the dominant role in a bondage game. Finally Walker finished his last beer and put the glass down (Colin was sipping a glass of water). "So shall we?" he asked, standing up. Colin smiled. He pushed his chair back and picked up a small rucksack that had been leaning against the leg of the table. "Yes, let's."

There's usually no shortage of cabs in London on a Monday night, and Walker was able to flag one down quickly. Smiling, he held open the door and Colin stepped inside. Walker got in beside him and leaned forward to give the driver the address; he didn't notice Colin – who'd been careful so far not to touch anything inside the cab – pull a pair of thin black leather gloves from his jacket pocket and unobtrusively slip them on.

Battersea, London; March 10, 1993

The caretaker was just finishing his morning rounds of the apartment block, already anticipating his lunch break, when he heard the dogs barking. He frowned, puzzled. That sounded like it was coming from Mr. Walker's flat. The bearded theater director lavished endless attention on his two dogs – a white German shepherd and a black Labrador – and every chance his busy schedule allowed he was walking them around the streets or the local park. Now that he thought about it, though, he didn't remember seeing him this morning. Or yesterday for that matter. Surely if Walker had had to go away unexpectedly he'd have said something, and not just left the dogs locked up? Concerned now, he knocked on the apartment door. The first knock was gentle, almost apologetic – he didn't like disturbing the residents at home if he could avoid it. The second, a minute later, was louder and more urgent. Apart from a renewed volley of frantic barks it brought no response. He stood there for a minute longer, turning the problem over in his mind, then came to a decision and fumbled in a pocket for his master key.

As soon as he stepped inside the apartment he knew something was badly wrong. The dogs, sensing a stranger's presence, were going absolutely wild now and the noise was coming from the spare bedroom – they'd been shut in there. The rest of the apartment had clearly been thoroughly searched – drawers pulled out and their contents rifled through, some of them dumped on the floor. With a feeling of dread, he walked slowly towards the door of the main bedroom and pushed it warily open.

Metropolitan Police CID, Wandsworth Station; March 10, 1993

Detective Inspector Martin Finnegan glanced at his watch when the phone rang; it was about 12:50pm. He picked up the receiver and gave his name. Minutes later he was racing out of his office, pulling on his jacket and calling for a team of detectives to get ready to move. A murder victim had been discovered, and from the initial report he'd received it was no ordinary killing – it was more grotesque and bizarre than anything he'd ever encountered before.

Finnegan and his team secured the Battersea apartment and questioned the caretaker, then made their way through the mess to the murder scene. The caretaker's panicked report had been accurate; the scene was utterly bizarre. Peter Walker lay on his bed, face up; abrasions on his wrists and ankles showed where he'd been fastened to the bed with rope and handcuffs. Only the feet could be seen, as a duvet covered most of the corpse. Placed on top were two teddy bears carefully arranged nose to groin in a "69" position. The scene was photographed from multiple angles, then gloved hands removed the bears and drew back the duvet. Now the full horror of the crime became apparent.

Walker had been savagely beaten as he lay helpless, tied to his own bed. Lash marks from a whip crisscrossed his torso among a sea of half-formed bruises. Gruesomely, he'd been gagged with a knotted condom. Another condom had been stretched over his nose. Finnegan stared unhappily at the vile tableau. It was already clear that he wasn't looking at a normal everyday murder. This atrocity was the work of a seriously deranged mind.

Chapter 1

Law enforcement agencies worldwide use standard behavioral checklists when they're looking for serial killers. Decades of research has found that this terrifying subclass of murderers carries a list of warning signs, and Colin Ireland's personal history flew quite a few of them.

Ireland was born in Dartford, Kent, on March 16, 1954. His mother, Pat Williams,[iii] was only seventeen years old and her boyfriend abandoned her not long after she gave birth. It goes without saying that her son had a difficult start in life. In his first six years the small family had to move home no less than nine times. Once, not long after he started school, he came home one day to find that his mother had moved unexpectedly. Concerned neighbors managed to track her down and reunite her with her young son, but it was clearly a completely dysfunctional upbringing. His mother was too young for the responsibility and not well educated; when she became pregnant she'd been an assistant in a small corner store. Bringing up a son was beyond her and although her parents helped out where they could Colin was neglected much of the time. He was also a small, skinny boy – "a runt", as he described himself - and suffered constant bullying at school, which didn't help his self-esteem or social skills.

Dartford is a slightly conflicted place. An ancient settlement – archaeologists have found traces of human habitation dating back more than 250,000 years – the town itself was founded sometime in the 5th century AD where the Roman military road crossed the River Darent. In the Middle Ages it developed into an industrial town powered by watermills along the river. When real industry arose in Britain, though, Dartford was swiftly eclipsed by the huge growth of London. The paper mills, cement factories and brewing industry went into decline and Dartford became a satellite of the capital. By the 1960s jobs in the town were scarce, and most people commuted into London to work. The city was like a magnet, drawing in people from the surrounding towns, and soon enough Ireland was drawn towards it too.

As a teenager Ireland, the skinny runt, suddenly hit a growth spurt. By the time he left school at the age of 13 he was rapidly growing into a powerful, bulky young man.[iv] With his new size and strength he managed to pick up a string of unskilled jobs in and around Dartford. Like many youths from a troubled background, though, he also gradually drifted into minor crime. Housebreaking and petty theft seemed like easy ways to supplement his income, but in the 1960s and 70s the British police were a lot less bureaucratic and more effective than a modern force. When Ireland stole £4 in 1970, planning to use the money to run away to London, he was quickly caught.

Finchton Manor was a private rehabilitative school, set up for boys from well-off families who had behavioral problems. It was quite selective and only accepted boys of above-average intelligence, and its method was to allow them to socialize and develop in an informal environment without much in the way of discipline and structure. Finchton was unconventional but highly successful – it's believed that several British politicians spent time there as boys, and so did some celebrities. One of them was musician Tom Robinson,[v] who would later become a prominent gay rights activist. The school could take troublesome youths and help them resolve their problems without shoveling them into the brutal maw of the criminal justice system, and that interested Kent County Council. It interested them enough that they paid for two places at the school, planning to use them to rehabilitate boys convicted of minor crimes. In 1970, they allocated one of those places to Colin Ireland.

It's interesting that the council chose Ireland for Finchton Manor. He hadn't been doing well at school and had left early, but clearly they'd decided he was more intelligent than his lackluster grades showed. Later events would suggest they were right – Ireland was unqualified but he had a sharp, analytical mind and a highly developed ability to plan and execute complex tasks. Finchton could have been just what he needed. Unfortunately, it didn't turn out well. There was almost instant conflict between the awkward council placement and the boys from rich families, and this quickly turned into bullying. Ireland had had enough of being bullied though. He'd endured it at school but he wasn't going to take it any longer. Outnumbered, he decided that facing up to his tormentors directly wouldn't help. Instead he singled out one of the ringleaders, heaped balls of newspaper around his belongings and set fire to the pile.[vi]

Finchton was used to behavior problems – solving them was why the school existed – but deliberate arson was too much. A staff member managed to put the fire out before any serious damage was done and the council was informed. That evening a social worker arrived to take Ireland away from the school. He didn't want to stay in council care though, and immediately carried through his original plan – he ran away to London.

Chapter 2

London; March 10, 1993

As a young Anglican vicar Chad Varah presided over the funeral of a 14-year-old girl who'd killed herself out of shame. She believed she'd caught a sexually transmitted disease from her boyfriend; in fact she'd been having her first period.[vii] Varah was appalled by the waste of a life and dedicated his career to sex education and suicide prevention. In 1952, he founded The Samaritans, a charity that gave despairing people someone to talk to. The organization places notices at popular jumping spots like Beachy Head, runs drop-in centers and trains prison volunteers, but the core of its work is a 24-hour helpline that's free to call from any UK number. It's obviously a successful concept because it's been taken up by similar groups around the world, like Contact USA, but it's hard to say exactly how many lives The Samaritans have saved – they operate a strict confidentiality code and only pass information to the emergency services under the most extreme circumstances. The volunteers who staff its call centers hear some appalling tales of human suffering and depravity; their effectiveness relies on their discretion. Now they were about to hear something they couldn't keep quiet.

Around 5:00pm – more than four hours after Walker's body was discovered, but before the police informed the media of the murder – a Samaritans volunteer answered an incoming call. He expected to hear a depressed or emotional person in need of someone to talk to; instead a brisk, efficient male voice reeled off an address in Battersea. Baffled, the volunteer asked what the address was for. The voice told him there were two dogs there and they'd been locked in a room for two days.[viii] This was an animal welfare issue; it wasn't what the helpline was for. The confused volunteer attempted to probe, wanting to know what this was all about - but then the caller, becoming agitated now, dropped his bombshell. The owner of the dogs was dead, because the caller had killed him.

The Samaritans' confidentiality rules were in place to protect vulnerable people; they didn't cover this. Within minutes of the call the volunteer was on the phone to Battersea Police Station, where DI Finnegan was puzzling over the murder that had been dropped in his lap. The detective deduced – correctly, as it turned out – that the killer had been worried at the lack of reporting and assumed Walker's corpse hadn't been found. There was little doubt that the caller had been Walker's murderer; while he hadn't given all the details he knew quite a lot about a crime that hadn't hit the media yet.

Barely an hour later any doubt was wiped away. Brandon Malinsky, a night news editor at popular tabloid newspaper *The Sun*, answered his phone and heard the same story as The Samaritans had, starting with the dogs then rapidly moving on to a confession to murder. This time the caller went into more detail, explaining that he'd made a New Year resolution to kill a gay man and had now acted on it. He mentioned that Walker had been tied up as part of a sex game; Malinsky was struck by how calm he sounded. It didn't sound like one of the raving cranks who plagued them and the veteran journalist decided he had to take it seriously. When the caller was finished he rang off; then, glancing at the list of phone numbers taped to the wall beside his desk, he placed a call to Scotland Yard. Two hours later the Met Police rang him back to confirm that everything the mysterious caller had said was true.

The problem for Finnegan and his team was that, apart from what the killer had said during his two calls, they knew very little about what had happened. They thought they knew why the killer had decorated the corpse with condoms – it was clear from the medications in the victim's cabinet that he'd been HIV-positive. That wasn't much to go on though. They weren't getting anywhere with tracking Walker's movements after he left work around 5:00pm on March 8 because nobody at The Coleherne was talking about what might have happened. The forensics team found that the apartment had been wiped for fingerprints or any other traces left behind by the killer. Walker had been secured to his bed with rope and handcuffs, but the restraints were now gone. The autopsy revealed that after being beaten the victim had been asphyxiated with a plastic grocery bag taken from his own kitchen.

The investigation soon discovered that cash had been withdrawn using Walker's bank and credit cards on the morning of March 9, hours after the estimated time of death, at an ATM not far from his apartment. From this they worked out – again, correctly – that the killer had tortured his victim into revealing the PIN codes for the cards. That was a potential lead and the missing cards were put on a watch list; if they were used again it might give a clue to the killer's location. What they didn't know was that the cards had been snapped in half and, along with Walker's keys, thrown from Battersea Bridge into the muddy depths of the Thames. Everything else used in the crime – rope, handcuffs, clothes and even gloves – had been packed into a rucksack and thrown from the window of a moving train, straight off a bridge and into the Regent's Canal in East London. The killer had systematically eliminated every physical clue that might have led the police to him. Peter Walker's last date had come out of nowhere, killed, and vanished.

May 28

The Coleherne, Earl's Court, London

Christopher Dunn had a secret. Five days a week he worked in a public library in Harrow, a respectable suburb in Northwest London. He lived in Wealdstone, an area of Harrow that was starting to see increasing problems from drugs and youth crime, but his own neighbors were conventional working- and lower middle class people with the innate conservatism of the English. They wouldn't approve of his secret, so he was very careful never to reveal it anywhere near his home.

Libraries have long opening hours and during the week it was often 9pm or later by the time Dunn got home, but this Friday he'd finished early and he planned to make the most of it. After work he'd showered and dressed, then headed into central London by train and Underground. From Earl's Court tube station he'd walked the last 400 yards to his favorite pub and now, just before 6pm, he was enjoying a pint of beer in the familiar surroundings of The Coleherne. This was his secret; unbeknown to his neighbors or co-workers Christopher Dunn was gay, and his preference was for masochistic bondage sex. The Coleherne was his refuge, the place where he could throw off his conventional façade for a while. It was one of the few places in London where he felt he could safely be what he was.

He hadn't been there long when another man, who'd just arrived and got himself a drink, approached his table. When he asked if he could sit down Dunn eyed him with interest. He didn't know the man, although he might have seen him before – he couldn't be sure. He'd certainly never spoken to him. Now he had the chance. "Sure, sit down," he said, "I'm Chris."

The big man took a seat across the table from him and held out his hand. "I'm Colin."

Wealdstone, London; May 30, 1993

Christopher Dunn maintained a quiet, conventional front to the world and most of his acquaintances had no idea about the secret life he'd built around The Coleherne. He wasn't reclusive though, and he had at least one friend who'd expected to speak to him over the weekend. When this friend hadn't heard anything by Sunday he tried calling; then, concerned, he went round to Dunn's neat little Victorian cottage. Finally he got the door open and looked inside. Minutes later he was dialing 999.

When the police arrived it was immediately obvious that this death wasn't going to go in the book as natural causes. The patrol officers called in detectives from the CID team at South Harrow Police Station, routine procedure in any cases of suspicious death - and this was definitely suspicious. Dunn's naked body was girdled by a studded belt, and he'd been gagged with a black leather harness obviously designed for the purpose. There were also burn marks around his testicles and fading lash marks on his torso. What there wasn't, was an obvious cause of death. In general terms, the detectives could see that Dunn had asphyxiated – oxygen deprivation leaves visible signs on the body. The question was, how?

The CID men went through Dunn's home carefully and thoroughly, looking for any signs of foul play. They found nothing. Once again the killer had sanitized the flat with clinical efficiency – and this time he was helped by the fact that the police weren't even sure there *was* a killer. Finally the detectives, baffled, concluded that Dunn had accidentally suffocated himself during a bondage session and that he'd probably been alone when he died. The most worrying aspect was the fact that he'd been burned before death. Even that could easily have been self-inflicted though and there was no sign that anyone else had been in the apartment. Relieved that this case could be closed, the DI wrote out his report suggesting accidental death as the most probable conclusion and shut it away in a drawer. The death had been odd enough that an autopsy and inquest would take place; if the body did show signs of criminal injury it would come out then.

What they didn't know was that Dunn, like Walker, had been robbed of his bank cards and forced to reveal the PINs to the killer. In fact, his testicles had been burned because one of the codes contained three consecutive identical numbers, and the assailant hadn't believed it was the real number; he'd applied the flame from a gas lighter as some extra persuasion. The cards were now gone and another rucksack, stuffed with clothes, rope and handcuffs, was settling into the mud under the waters of the Regent's Canal.

Chapter 3

Homeless and unqualified, the sixteen-year-old Colin Ireland faced a struggle to survive in London. He picked up odd jobs where he could and begged on the streets. For support he hung around with other homeless teenagers, including a group who frequently begged around the Playland arcade in Piccadilly Circus.[ix] Ireland stayed on the fringes of this group, never becoming fully involved, and part of the reason for that was that it was a frequent target for child molesters. A loose organization of pedophiles preyed on the boys around Playland, some of whom were willing to exchange sex for money or even just a bed for the night. Ireland never succumbed to that temptation but he did get offered. He was repelled and furious.

Unwilling to prostitute himself Ireland looked for another way to supplement his irregular pay packets and once again he turned to theft. He didn't do any better than he had first time round and again he was soon caught. The offence was more serious this time however – in early 1971 he was convicted of burgling a home. With his previous record that meant detention was inevitable despite his young age and this time there would be no private school as an easy option.

The British penal system realized a long time ago that there's a better chance of rehabilitating young offenders if they're not locked up alongside hardened adult criminals. The first specialized institution for boys and young men aged under 21 was set up in 1902 near the village of Borstal, only twelve miles from Ireland's birthplace in Dartford. By 1908, there were a string of them throughout Britain, all taking their name from the first. The main function of adult prisons was to keep criminals out of society but the borstals focused on education, in the hope their young inmates could be turned into productive citizens. They were still tough places though, with strict discipline and hard work. Ireland, convicted of burglary, soon found himself sent to one.

Despite the almost military-style discipline the borstals still suffered from many of the problems of any prison – hierarchies formed among the inmates, and those at the bottom of the pecking order were often mercilessly bullied. You could survive by being accepted by one of the ruling cliques or just persuading the others to leave you alone, but either way you had to be prepared to fight. Ireland had suffered enough bullying at school when he was small and weak; as his behavior at Finchton Manor had already shown he wasn't going to take any more. Fighting back was an option but there was another one, and it was easier. The institution he'd been sent to, Hollesley Bay in Suffolk, was an open borstal intended for boys who presented a low escape risk. Ireland had been assessed as falling into that category, but the prison service had been wrong. Quickly tiring of life inside Ireland simply walked out early one summer morning. To evade the initial search he hid in long grass in a corner of a field, lying there with no food or water until night fell. Then he set off into the flat Suffolk countryside.

Unfortunately for Ireland he'd misjudged the intensity of the search, and in a largely rural, agricultural county like Suffolk a strange teenager was conspicuous. Within days he was picked up by the police. He was also reassigned – as a proven escaper there would be no return to the easy regime at Hollesley Bay. Instead, he was moved to a more secure borstal, first Rochester and then Grendon. Finally, he was released, aged eighteen, in mid-1972.

By Ireland's own account, he had few memories of the next few years. He drifted, more or less aimlessly, through southern England. He still picked up odd jobs when he could. When he couldn't, he stole. In 1975, he got caught again. This time he was 21 and no longer considered a young offender, so when a London court found him guilty of an array of offences including burglary, property damage and stealing a car he was sentenced to detention in an adult prison. In the end he served a year of an 18-month sentence. The first few months were in overcrowded city jails where the guards, under serious pressure, had no time to get to know the inmates; Ireland said that during this period he started to believe his name was "Oi, you". Later he was moved to Lewes Prison in East Sussex. This was more modern and spacious than the grim Victorian cell blocks he'd been incarcerated in and the guards had more time to make some attempt at rehabilitation. On his first morning in the prison Ireland was astonished to be greeted with "Good morning, Colin".[x]

As far as rehabilitation went, though, Ireland may already have been a lost cause by this point. He'd had two chances to turn his life around in institutions for young offenders and he'd thrown them both away. The shock of adult prison might have managed to deter him before he drifted even further from the rest of society, but it clearly wasn't working.

Released in November 1976 Ireland ended up living in Swindon, 60 miles west of London. Here he had his first serious relationship with a woman, a mother of four from the West Indies who'd immigrated to Britain as a teenager. She was five years older than Ireland but they lived together for a few months and even discussed marriage. The plans came to nothing though – before long he was back in prison, this time for "demanding with menace". That earned him another eighteen months. Just months after his release he was back inside; two years for robbery, of which he served a year. In between sentences he worked at a variety of jobs. With his size and bulk he did well as a nightclub bouncer, including a stint at one Swindon gay club. He joined the Auxiliary Fire Service as a part-time volunteer firefighter. After the sentence for robbery he found a position as a chef at a London restaurant. It was at that point that he probably came closest to turning his life around.

In the early and mid-1980s there was a surge of interest in survivalism in the UK. Probably prompted by the fear of nuclear war, it lacked the political ideology shared by many US survivalists and concentrated solely on self-reliance skills. Clubs developed in many large cities where people would share survival and improvisation tips, then spend weekends in the woods trying them out. Sometime in 1981 Ireland developed an interest in this hobby and started attending meetings. He'd already tried to join the French Foreign Legion and been rejected because of his criminal record; the Legion might once have been a refuge for men on the run from the law, but those days are long gone. He enjoyed military trappings though, and photographs taken during weekends living rough show him dressed in surplus British Army combat gear.

Many newspaper reports claim that Ireland was a former British soldier, but that's not true – his record would have barred him from enlistment even if he had ever applied, which he didn't. It's likely that journalists saw those photos of him in a camouflaged jacket and made a false assumption. He was enthusiastic about survival training although his dedication to the idea of self-reliance has been questioned. Some people who knew him at that time claim he used to sneak into nearby towns to buy food when he got tired of trapping rabbits and foraging for edible mushrooms, but he was a regular attender for a while. At one lecture, he met 36-year-old Virginia Zammit.

Zammit had been left paralyzed from the waist down after a traffic accident twelve years earlier, and she often found life frustrating. Previously active and interested in the outdoors she hated that people saw the wheelchair she sat in and barely noticed her as a person. Ireland was different. For the first time in several years she felt appreciated for who she was and a relationship quickly sprang up between the two. In 1982 they were married, and it seemed that Ireland might finally have managed to turn his life around. He adored Zammit's five-year-old daughter and would spend hours playing with her. Zammit herself worked in a local elementary school and Ireland started volunteering there, displaying an unsuspected talent for helping children learn to read and draw. The couple lived on a housing estate in Holloway, a working-class district in central London, and around the area Ireland became known as "the gentle giant".

Under the surface, things weren't looking so good though. Within months of the wedding Ireland was sentenced to eight weeks in jail for attempted deception. In 1985, he got six months for "going equipped to cheat". His gentle behavior also began to change, and he was increasingly aggressive. Then in 1987 he had an affair with another woman, and Zammit found out. They were divorced shortly afterwards.

Chapter 4

London is one of the world's great cities. Over 15 million people – a quarter of the entire UK population – live in the London metro area and close to 8.5 million in the city itself. Apart from the famous Square Mile of the City of London financial district, which has its own police force, law enforcement across this bustling megacity is the responsibility of the Metropolitan Police. It's far too large for a single force to operate across it though, so the Met is split into operational divisions. In 1993, there were five of them and while they all reported to the force headquarters at New Scotland Yard they had a lot of autonomy. That made it easier for them to get on with day to day policing tasks but it also had its drawbacks. The divisions talked to each other regularly, but IT systems were a lot less developed in 1993 and data was shared between divisions much more slowly than it is now.

Because Walker and Dunn had died in different divisions, the deaths were being investigated by different teams of detectives. Harrow CID were waiting for the autopsy results to confirm the cause of death but had tentatively filed it as an accident; if they'd been aware of Walker's death ten weeks earlier it's likely they would have seen it as a probable murder instead, but that information wasn't at their fingertips. Meanwhile, Detective Inspector Finnegan's investigation into the Walker case had stalled. As well as the cleanup that had removed physical evidence from the murder scene they were facing a wall of silence from the most likely witnesses to the events leading up to the crime.

Until 1967 even consensual sex between two men was a criminal offence in the United Kingdom – high-profile victims of the law included writer Oscar Wilde and mathematician Alan Turing. The Sexual Offences Act 1967 brought in limited decriminalization under certain circumstances; the sex had to be fully consensual, between two men aged 21 or over – five years higher than the age of consent for straight sex – and conducted in private. It was a step forward for LGBT rights in England and Wales (Scotland and Northern Ireland have their own legal systems) but in many ways not a large one. Huge swathes of the legal system still disapproved of gay relationships and applied the law in a very narrow way. The "in private" clause was used to prosecute anyone engaging in sex that involved more than two people, to gays who met in hotel rooms and even to anything that happened in a private home if a third person was somewhere else in the house. Unsurprisingly the result was that many gay men distrusted and feared the police, and were very reluctant to talk to them. It didn't help that the day after Walker's body had been found the Law Lords – at the time the UK's highest court – had ruled that consensual BDSM activity was still a crime. For the clientele of The Coleherne that meant talking to the Met was the last thing they wanted to do; they were far too likely to end up being arrested themselves.

From the point of view of the police, the leather and BDSM subculture was a complete mystery to them. Its members were significantly more likely to be murdered than the general population but many of these crimes were mistaken for accidental deaths resulting from a bondage game gone wrong. Too many officers also had a distaste for the lifestyle that made them unenthusiastic when it came to investigating crimes against gays. For those cops it was tempting, where murder was in doubt, to write it off as an accidental choking death and close the file. Attitudes within the Met were slowly changing, although not fast enough for many in the gay community, but even those officers who were sympathetic were hampered by a lack of understanding. While street coppers and detectives had an encyclopedic knowledge of mainstream London life and the city's diverse neighborhoods they simply didn't know how things were done among the BDSM crowd.

June 4

Old Brompton Road, London

Perry Bradley III liked London. The ancient city, with its blend of classical and modern buildings and patchwork mix of diverse neighborhoods, was very different from his childhood sixty miles from Dallas. He was the son of Perry Bradley Jr., a successful fundraiser for the Democratic Party, and his upbringing was a privileged one with all the benefits that wealth and social status can bring. He'd had the best of care and the best of schools, as well as an easy introduction to the upper levels of Texas society. In return he was expected to make a name for himself in business or politics, and find himself a suitable wife. From his late teens his mother had started playing the mating game, hooking him up with the daughters of her friends, but he'd been unenthusiastic. Long before the round of arranged dates and carefully selected parties began he'd felt that he was somehow different, and by his early teens he had known he was gay. In the conservative society of Hopkins County that was awkward, and he knew his parents would be horrified, so he'd kept it to himself. He'd even feigned enthusiasm for his mother's matchmaking and it amused him that he'd done that so successfully – he had a reputation for being interested in pretty girls. That had kept everyone satisfied for a while but when he graduated from college without a steady girlfriend the hints started to get heavier. It was a relief when he found a management post with adhesive manufacturer J-B Weld and moved away.

Now, at the age of 35, he was J-B Weld's international sales director and spent a lot of time developing the UK market. He was loving it. Gay rights in the UK might not be as universal as they could have been, but British law was still a lot more relaxed than it was at home – Texas still had a sodomy law that explicitly banned sex between two men and the Supreme Court had upheld it just a few years earlier. Any relationship he had in Dallas could result in a lot more than parental disapproval; it could mean jail. That wouldn't happen here, so he enjoyed the glorious feeling of liberation as he pushed open the door of The Coleherne and stepped inside.

It was a pleasant early summer evening, and fairly warm by London standards – 73° Fahrenheit. Bradley had enjoyed the mile's walk from his luxury apartment in Kensington; he didn't miss the stifling heat and humidity of Texas any more than he missed the homophobia, and while the English complained about the heat he found it very pleasant. Not wanting to waste this rare taste of summer he got himself a drink and took it out to the beer garden behind the pub. Sitting down at one of the tables he glanced at his watch – he'd arranged to meet up with a man he'd chatted to the week before and was keen to see how it would work out, but he didn't expect him for another half hour. He leaned back in his chair, enjoying sunshine and beer.

He'd only been there a few minutes when another man walked over to his table and asked if he could sit down. Bradley studied him for a moment before replying. Well, he had to admit it to himself - he was tempted. The newcomer was tall and well built, just the type he liked. It was with real regret that he shook his head. "I'm really sorry, I'm supposed to be meeting a friend," he said apologetically, "Catch you later?"

The stranger nodded amiably enough. "Sure." He waved his glass in a friendly gesture and wandered off into the bar.

Bradley settled back down to wait, contentedly sipping his beer and looking round the garden. As time passed, though, he found himself watching the door to the bar more and more often. He glanced at his watch. A few minutes later he checked it again, frowning. He'd expected his date to be here by now. It looked like he wouldn't be making it. Bradley gave it a few minutes more then finished his pint and stood up.

Leaning against the old bar, Bradley sipped a fresh beer and scanned the pub's interior. Finally he spotted the man he was looking for, sitting alone at a table in the back corner. Casually he wandered over, hoping his earlier rebuff wasn't about to be reciprocated. "Hey, sorry about earlier," he said, "Looks like I'm on my own after all. Is it okay if I join you this time?"

He was rewarded with a friendly smile. "Sure, go ahead. I know how it is sometimes. Haven't seen you around before. You're American? On holiday?"

Bradley smiled. "American yes, on vacation no. I work here." He pulled out a chair then extended his hand. "Perry."

"Pleased to meet you. I'm Colin." The big man nudged his rucksack out of the way with a foot. "Sit down."

Kensington, London

Bradley unlocked the door of his apartment and waved Colin inside. The Englishman looked around appreciatively. "Nice place you have here." At Bradley's invitation he sat down, dropping his rucksack at his feet.

Bradley shrugged out of his jacket. "Say, I'm kind of hungry. You want something to eat?"

An hour later, after a light meal and a glass of wine, Bradley suggested they move to the bedroom. Colin stood and followed him through, but as Bradley reached for his belt he hesitated. "Look, uh… can I ask you something?"

"Sure, go ahead."

"Is it alright if I tie you up first?"

Bradley wasn't so sure about that. He liked The Coleherne and the men who frequented it, but bondage really wasn't his thing. He gently declined. Colin didn't let it rest though. Awkwardly, he explained that without an element of sadomasochism he could never get aroused. The American nodded understandingly. "Hey, sure, if that's what it takes. Let me look for some old ties or something."

"That's no problem. I've got some gear in here." He patted the rucksack that he'd casually brought from the living room and gave a lopsided grin. "Never know when you'll get lucky, eh?"

Bradley laughed. "Good way to look at it." He started to unbutton his shirt. "Go on then, buddy, do your worst."

Five minutes later Bradley, nude, was securely bound and lying face down on his bed. Despite himself he felt a shiver of anticipation. This really wasn't his scene but the quick, proficient way the big man had trussed him was strangely exciting. It made him seem so dominant and masterful...Perry Bradley waited for what came next as Colin knelt beside the bed.

He leaned in and placed his lips close to the helpless American's ear. "Right, this isn't what you expected," he murmured, "but it's happening, and there's not a lot you can do about it."

In the circumstances Bradley remained remarkably calm. "So, what happens now?" he asked.

"I'm a professional thief, and believe me I'll do anything to get money. I've tortured people to get what I want, and I'll start hurting you…"

Bradley was surprised to realize that he actually found these words reassuring. He was rich; robbery was always a threat. So far he'd been lucky and if his luck had run out, well, this way was probably better than most. The Englishman had talked him into being tied him up, but if he'd meant any harm he was big and powerful enough to have subdued Bradley the moment they walked into the apartment. All the signs said this was crime for gain, not anything personal. He lay helpless on his bed, listening as Colin expertly searched the apartment. Yes, he acted like a professional. Not good news, of course, but it could be a lot worse…

He couldn't keep track of time and his watch was out of sight on the floor. Minutes passed. The sounds of the thorough, efficient pillaging moved from room to room. Eventually Colin returned. He held up a fistful of cards and bills. "A hundred quid. Any more stashed away?"

Bradley shook his head. "No, that's it," he said truthfully. "I don't have any more cash."

"That better be true. I'll look again before I go, and if I find anything that would be bad news for you. Now, the cards. Tell me the codes."

"Sure, I'll give you what you want. I'll go get you the money myself if you want."

Colin shook his head. "No. I won't allow it. Just give me the numbers." He pulled out a sheet of paper and waited, pen poised, for Bradley to do so. He did. Why take the chance that this man would follow through on his threat of torture?

With the information he wanted tucked away in his pocket Colin went round the apartment switching off the lights. Returning to the bedroom he pulled out a chair and sat down. He turned the radio on, fiddled with the dial until he found a late-night discussion show and lowered the volume to a discreet level, then made himself comfortable. Finally he said to Bradley, "It's going to be a long night. Get some sleep if you can."

That seemed like a tall order. He was sprawled helpless and naked on his bed, wrists cuffed behind him and ankles tied together. It wasn't all that uncomfortable – when he'd been secured it had still been under the pretense of a game, so his captor had been quite considerate – but he was in a frightening position. He lay there in the dark, his mind endlessly picking away at the situation he was in. Again he had no idea how much time passed but suddenly, almost unbelievably, he realized he was having trouble keeping his eyes open. For a few minutes he fought to stay awake, then gave up. Colin had said he should try to get some sleep, so why not? It wasn't like staying awake was going to help him, was it? He let his eyelids close and drifted off. In the chair a few feet away the other man frowned thoughtfully at the wall, as if struggling with some internal dilemma.

Bradley barely stirred as the noose was slipped gently over his head but he jerked awake moments later, at the shock of the rope tightening round his throat. Bleary from sleep it was seconds before he realized what was happening to him; he didn't even begin to wonder why. By the time he understood what was happening the rope was already biting into his windpipe and the sides of his neck, starving his lungs of air and his brain of oxygenated blood. The room was weakly lit by the orange streetlamp glow that filtered in around the curtains but now even that was rapidly fading, blackness gathering round the edges of his vision and swiftly narrowing it down to a tunnel. He tried to struggle for a moment but only managed to writhe uselessly against the cuffs and the closing noose. He gave up and lay there passively as the darkness claimed him.

It had been a warm evening when Perry Bradley made his last visit to The Coleherne and for the next few days the temperature continued to rise. June 7 was the hottest day of the year so far (and ended up as one of the five hottest overall) and by early afternoon it was obvious to the residents of the Kensington apartment block that something was badly wrong in that nice young American's flat. The doorbell rang unanswered and, dreading what the smell suggested, they called the police.

Chapter 5

Janet Young first saw Colin Ireland in late August 1989, when he walked in the door of her pub. He filled the doorway, she remembered; all conversation stopped and every head turned to look at him.[xi] Ireland didn't seem to mind. He walked up to the bar and asked Janet if she had any of her bed and breakfast rooms available. She did, unfortunately for her.

The Globe is an 18th century inn in the small Devon town of Buckfastleigh, and Janet – a single parent with two children aged eleven and thirteen – was struggling to run it on her own. Devon is a popular tourist destination but Buckfastleigh isn't one of its leading resorts. There are a few attractions near the town – an otter sanctuary, a butterfly farm and a heritage railway – but nothing to hold visitors there for more than a few hours. Its biggest claims to fame are a local legend that inspired the Sherlock Holmes story *The Hound of the Baskervilles*, and a Benedictine monastery notorious for producing a vile, caffeine-laced fortified wine – 90 per cent of which is drunk by violent teenage delinquents 500 miles away on the outskirts of Glasgow. The ancient, narrow streets are lined with private homes, small stores and a remarkable number of pubs (there are seven – one for every 500 inhabitants). Most of the pubs have a few rooms to let but the business they get is mostly transient. Tourists might stop for lunch and one or two drinks but most of the evening trade is local people. Occasionally cavers stay for a day or two – the surrounding limestone is riddled with caverns and some of them are spectacular. One not far from the town, Joint Mitnor Cave, still has the remains of exotic animals that roamed Britain tens of thousands of years ago. The elephants, hippos and hyenas that died there aren't even fossilized; their skeletons have been preserved by the sheltering rock.

Three miles west of town the neatly tended fields and dairy herds fade out into the wilderness of Dartmoor, 400 square miles of rocky summits, rolling windswept grassland and peat bogs. On a sunny day the scenery is spectacular but mostly it's a bleak place and dangerous for the unwary. In the 1980s it was a popular destination for survivalists eager to test their outdoor skills, as well as being a regular training ground for the Royal Marine Commandos. Ireland had traveled to Devon to spend time out on the moor; he aimed to make long expeditions into the harsh expanse, living off the land and building his own shelters to protect him from the elements.

That was the plan, at least. Janet recalls, "He was gonna go out all night and catch a rabbit and all this sort of thing. But actually he wasn't very good at it and he always came home for his tea."[xii]

Janet didn't mind though. By her own admission she was feeling vulnerable at the time and Ireland, always willing to help out around the place, swept her off her feet. Within a week of his arrival he was living with her in her apartment above the bar, and in December 1989 they were married. What she didn't realize was that her new husband was extremely controlling – she was too grateful for his help around the pub to notice how rapidly he was taking over all the key decisions – and, by this point, increasingly unstable. It wasn't long before his façade of normality began to crack and a darker side showed through. One night, after an argument, he threw her out of their bedroom. When she moved to another one he followed her, smashed the lamp and stalked her round the dark room, taunting her.

Despite these worrying moments Janet – and her children, who'd quickly become extremely attached to Ireland – believed the relationship was generally going quite well. Over Easter 1990 a spike in tourism meant the pub was extremely busy for several days and Ireland's help was invaluable to her. After the holiday, when things quieted down again, they agreed to take a break and get away for a few days. Janet wanted to take the children to visit friends in London and Ireland said he'd spend the weekend in Southend-On-Sea where he had friends of his own.

On Sunday Janet waited with the children for Ireland, who'd taken her car, to pick them up. He was late, and eventually she grew concerned. Thinking that perhaps he'd had an accident she called the pub to see if anyone had heard anything – and was hit with a shocking revelation. Hours after dropping her off in London Ireland had reappeared at the Globe. He'd told the barmaid that bailiffs had threatened to repossess some of Janet's possessions to repay a debt, and he was going to take them to a safe place. That sounded believable enough that nobody interfered as he packed up most of her belongings, loaded them into the car and drove off. He'd already emptied her bank accounts; now he simply disappeared. Janet never heard from him again, and the next time she saw his face it was on the evening news.

Chapter 6

The Metropolitan Police now had three files open, each of them involving a gay man who'd been found dead with signs of having been tied up; in two of the cases there were visible signs of strangulation on the corpse. Even so nobody had made a connection between them. Peter Walker's death was being investigated by Battersea CID, who'd run into a wall of silence from the gay community and made no progress at all since March. Christopher Dunn fell under the Harrow police area – and had been written up as a probable accident - and now Perry Bradley's death, clearly a homicide, was baffling the detectives at Kensington Station. In fact the Kensington team was extremely close to the unsuspected killer's hunting ground – their station, a 1960s brick monstrosity, was barely a thousand yards north of The Coleherne.

That wasn't helping them though. As DI Finnegan from Battersea had already found out nobody in the BDSM scene wanted to talk to the police for fear of ending up in court on indecency charges, and in any case they didn't even know for sure if Bradley had been gay. They'd been in touch with his family, who insisted that he wasn't, but they'd also tracked down and talked to many of his friends in London and so they were "keeping an open mind" about his sexuality.[xiii]

Forensic investigation of Bradley's apartment came up, unsurprisingly, with nothing. Yet again the scene had been thoroughly wiped down and sanitized. Bradley's credit cards - £200 had been withdrawn the day after he died – had been destroyed and clothes, handcuffs and rope were at the bottom of the Regent's Canal. This time the rucksack also contained a plate, a wine glass and a handful of flatware from the meal the two men had shared before the nightmare began. They'd carried fingerprints and, while they could have been wiped clean, they would still have suggested to police that Bradley had been killed by someone he'd invited in. With a single dirty plate on the table it left open the possibility that an intruder had invaded the apartment to rob and kill, weakening the chain leading back to the pub garden where the fatal seduction had really taken place.

The failure to link the three deaths meant that, at this point, the police had no idea at all what they were dealing with. If they had known it would have made their job much easier. While a serial killer is a frightening prospect for law enforcement because the chances are he'll kill again and again until he's stopped, at least with a string of linked murders they can start to look for patterns and shared features; that's their best chance of finding a lead, because eventually almost every killer makes a mistake. Looked at in isolation, though – and that's what was happening – each of the murders was baffling and frustrating.

If the Met were frustrated they weren't the only ones. Miles to the east of London, in the coastal resort of Southend-On-Sea, Colin Ireland was also growing exasperated. What was *wrong* with the police, he asked himself. Why weren't they linking the murders? Why hadn't they announced that a serial killer was stalking London's gay community? He couldn't understand it at all.

June 7

Old Brompton Street, London

Andrew Collier had no idea he was walking into an ambush. Like so many London BDSM devotees the old pub in Earl's Court was a sanctuary for him. He had an apartment in a housing complex for retirees, where he worked as caretaker, and he didn't need to hide his sexuality there; all the residents knew he was "the other way" and they didn't seem to care. In fact like many gay men he found that old ladies seemed to take a maternal interest in his well-being and kept him supplied with a constant stream of cakes, tea and news of how their grandchildren were getting on. He smiled faintly as he walked into the pub, thinking that he was lucky his job kept him so active; otherwise, with all those cakes, he'd be lucky to fit through the door.

Ordering himself a pint, he dropped a pound coin into the jukebox and punched in five selections before looking for a seat. It was a Monday night and while The Coleherne was never exactly empty it wasn't as crowded as it would be on the weekend, so he had a choice. Finally he settled on a table that gave him a good view of the door, and settled down to wait for someone interesting.

When the tall, broad-shouldered man walked in Collier checked him out with interest. He looked vaguely familiar – he was sure he'd seen him a couple of times before. He didn't recall him having a regular partner though, not that that was surprising in the freewheeling culture of The Coleherne. Well, it made him a possibility. The newcomer headed for the bar, nodding familiarly to one or two people as he went, and spoke to the barman. A minute later, pint in hand, he turned to look around for a seat. Collier made a decision; he caught the man's eye, then smiled and raised his beer invitingly. The big man smiled back and began to weave his way towards him through the scattered drinkers.

To Collier's pleasure his new companion seemed genuinely interested in him. He introduced himself as Colin and said he worked in a homeless shelter in Southend. That explained the small rucksack propped against the leg of his chair – the last train was just after midnight and if he met someone then of course he'd need an overnight bag. He smiled to himself. Well, that was fine. There was nothing wrong with showing a bit of optimism.

It didn't take long to come to an arrangement. Collier was well aware that his lifestyle could be risky, but he figured he'd become a pretty good judge of character over the years and he was happy to invite this man home with him – he didn't look like trouble.

Dalston, Northeast London

Collier's apartment was small and neat. He directed his guest to a chair, then shooed his cat Millie out of the way and sat down. Sipping a glass of water – he'd already had two beers and was wary of drinking too much, in case it interfered with his medication – he chatted casually for a while, putting his visitor at ease. He did seem slightly tense. Well, that wasn't too strange. After all he was in a stranger's home. Collier himself was relaxed and enjoying himself. The only worry was the matter of his HIV status. How should he mention that? Not everybody was understanding about it and he didn't want a scene.

Then they were interrupted by someone who clearly did want a scene. The muffled sound of passers-by talking outside suddenly swelled into a shouted argument. Collier chased Millie off his lap, stood and walked to the window. Twitching the curtain to one side he saw two young men quarreling in the street. It seemed to be just raised voices though. He watched for a minute but it didn't look like it was escalating into a fight. Then he sensed movement as Colin came up behind him; the big man rested one hand lightly on a metal rail that ran across the window just above the sill and looked over Collier's shoulder. "Drunk idiots, eh? You get them everywhere."

Collier turned round. "Sad but true," he said. "Anyway, it's getting late. Bedtime?"

Maybe he hadn't been such a good judge of character after all, he decided. Everything had gone as he expected until the handcuffs snapped closed and the last knot was tightened, but it had all been downhill from there. Now Colin was leaning over him, menacingly demanding the PIN code for his bank card. He might have made a misjudgment of his own though, Collier thought. He was no coward, and even tied up like this he wasn't just going to cave in. "Fuck off," he snarled angrily. "I can't stop you taking the cash but that's your lot."

Colin shrugged. "We'll see," he said. "Amazing how chatty people can get." He pulled a lighter from his pocket and thumbed the wheel. Moments later Collier was screaming into the pillow as the flame seared his testicles. "Feel like talking yet?"

"Fuck you!"

"No? Fine." The lighter scraped again and the pain came back.

He could hardly think straight now. Terror and rage mingled into a whirling turmoil of thoughts and images. When the flame or a lit cigarette was applied to his skin Colin muffled his face with the pillow to stifle his screams. Then he'd release the pressure and repeat his demand. Collier would sob out a bitter refusal and the process would start again. Finally, exhausted, he collapsed into semi consciousness. The torturer straightened up. "I'll leave you to think about it for a few minutes," he said. "Let's see if you have any more cash tucked away."

As Colin worked his way from room to room Collier lay slumped, listening to the sounds of drawers being pulled out and cupboards pillaged. Finally the search moved into his small storeroom, where many of his belongings were kept. He heard some boxes being emptied out, the clatter of small bottles bouncing on the floor, then a moment of silence – followed by a furious oath. He moaned in despair. It sounded like Colin had found his HIV medication.

He had. A minute later he burst into the bedroom, his face contorted with rage. "What the hell are you playing at?" he snarled. "You've got bloody AIDS and you weren't going to tell me? For fuck's sake! Spreading your fucking virus like that, it's outrageous! Well, I'll teach you." He raised his hands. In one was a length of rope. In the other, struggling furiously, was Millie the cat.

Collier's building was a quiet one with elderly residents and, at first, nobody noticed that he wasn't working. Through Tuesday he lay in his silent apartment. By Wednesday morning people were starting to wonder where he was, and the weather was also taking a hand. June 8 had been the hottest day of 1993, with temperatures passing 80° Fahrenheit. June 9 was the second hottest. Old men passing the end of the narrow corridor that led to Collier's front door paused, frowning as they caught a scent they hadn't smelled since the war. Memories of what caused that smell rose up from the dark places in their memories. Before long one of them called the police.

By the time the officers from Dalston Station broke in the door they were already pretty sure Collier was dead – the smell was unmistakable. What they weren't expecting was the scene that confronted them in the bedroom. This was by far the most gruesome tableau yet. They didn't even bother checking for signs of life; instead they retreated, preserving the crime scene – and getting away from the appalling sight – and radioed for CID. Even the hardened detectives were horrified at the calculated brutality of what they found and the ripples of shock spread out through the Met. Within hours a special team had been assigned to the case.

Detective Chief Inspector Albert Patrick was one of CID's bulldogs. A craggy-featured Scotsman, with a straightforward approach to policing not a million miles away from the BBC drama hero DCI Gene Hunt, he wasn't easily shocked. Later as Detective Superintendent he would rise to a senior position in the Flying Squad, the feared anti-armed-robbery unit known to London's villains as "The Sweeney". Even Patrick was surprised by what he found in the Dalston apartment. Collier's body lay on its back, ligature marks still visible in the swollen flesh of the wrists, ankles and neck. The testicles had been scorched and cigarette burns on his chest indicated prolonged torture. Gruesomely, Millie's limp corpse was stretched out on his chest with her jaws clamped round Collier's penis and her tail in his mouth. Condoms had been unrolled over tail and penis. Examinations showed that both had been strangled with a rope (in fact Millie had been hanged with a noose thrown over the bedroom door). DCI Patrick surveyed the freakish scene for a few minutes then turned to Detective Sergeant Terry Webster, who was standing stunned at his side. "Well look at that, Sergeant. That's unusual."

It certainly was unusual, and Patrick was instantly suspicious. He didn't believe that any killing as elaborate and ritualistic as this could be a one-off. He feared that either a serial killer had just launched his career or one had already been operating without being noticed. To find out, he assigned Webster to contact every CID office in London and find out about any recent murders that shared the same characteristics. Meanwhile the forensics team started an inch-by-inch examination of Collier's apartment.

Chapter 7

After Colin Ireland disappeared from Janet Young's life just after Easter 1990 he dropped out of sight for a while, but by early 1992 he was working in a shelter for the homeless in Southend-On-Sea. There was a certain irony in this, because for much of the time he worked there he was homeless himself. Amazingly, though, he was a competent and effective worker. The people who used the shelter liked him; he understood their situation, he sympathized with them and he wasn't judgmental about choices they'd made that had put them on the streets.

Shelter manager Richard Higgs soon came to appreciate the big, quiet man as a valued member of staff. He got on fairly well with him personally, too. Ireland could be moody sometimes, and on occasion he said startling things – once, when they were discussing how to remove a troublesome guest from the shelter, Ireland said "Well, I could stuff a few snooker balls down his throat" – but Higgs wrote that off as an inappropriate sense of humor. Mostly he felt sorry for him. Ireland revealed almost nothing about his past and when he did the stories were not happy ones. He told Higgs about coming home from elementary school to find his mother had moved, for example.[xiv] Given these hints of an unhappy background and his good work at the shelter it's not surprising Higgs was sympathetic; he had no idea of the depth of callousness Ireland could display.

Not everyone at the shelter felt the same way as Higgs, though. In early December 1992 he started to hear allegations that Ireland was groping female residents. These complaints weren't coming from the alleged victims – the source was other members of staff. Higgs didn't believe the accusations; even now, after all that happened, he thinks that in this case Ireland really was innocent and fell victim to a conspiracy among other employees. Is that true? It's hard to say, but Ireland was popular with the residents and it was only staff that made the allegations, so it's not unlikely. However, the campaign against him soon poisoned the atmosphere at work and within a couple of weeks Ireland was pressured into resigning. Higgs was sorry to see him go.

At this point Ireland was living in a rooming house in Southend, which was a step up from a homeless shelter or the streets but meant he had bills to pay. He did manage to find another job within a few days but he hated it. It was dull and menial; he spent all day breaking up old shipping pallets for recycling. It's possible that he'd finally developed a sense of achievement working in the shelter that might have given him another chance to make something worthwhile of his life, but now it had been snatched out from under him and he was, if not at rock bottom, pretty close to it. He fell into a depression; Higgs thought he seemed lost.

Lost he may have been; he was definitely profoundly unhappy and discontented with his life. Everything he'd attempted, he thought, had been a failure – it's hard to say if he had the self-awareness to realize that many of these failures had been his own fault. Now he was determined to make a name for himself in any way he could. If he couldn't be successful, he decided, he'd be notorious. After a miserable Christmas in his shabby room he made that fateful New Year resolution. He was going to achieve fame and recognition by killing, and he was going to target gay men.

Chapter 8

Albert Patrick's intuition had, for the first time, brought the Met close to the truth of what they were facing and he'd tasked his sergeant to search the recent murder files for evidence of a series. DS Webster set to work combing through the list of every murder in London over the last year. There had been more than 150, but many could be ruled out – all those where the killer had already been caught, domestic violence cases and gang deaths, for a start. Patrick told him to take an even narrower focus. Only crimes where the victim had been a gay man needed closer examination, and the signs they were looking for were restraint marks on the ankles and wrists, strangulation or asphyxiation and signs of abuse or torture before death. That excluded most of the unsolved cases until finally he was left with two that seemed likely. First he called Kensington Station to ask for more information about Perry Bradley. No, he was told, not related – Bradley wasn't gay. He was, of course, but the family were denying that and Kensington had decided to play along. Maintaining the façade in public was one thing though – misleading other investigators had much more serious consequences. Christopher Dunn should have been next on the list but his case was still marked as an accident.

Then Webster called DI Finnegan at Battersea to discuss Peter Walker, and finally he started to get somewhere. There was a list of similarities between the two cases; both gay, both tied up, both tortured – Walker by beating and whipping, Collier by burning. Most convincingly of all both had other items posed on top of them – Walker's soft toys and Millie's body – and both had condoms in their mouths and elsewhere on the corpse. That seemed to confirm Patrick's suspicions; the use of condoms in that way was just too unusual. In fact he'd never heard of it before.

Meanwhile the forensic team were scouring Collier's apartment for clues. It was a frustrating task at first. They quickly found that every surface had been wiped down. The ropes and handcuffs that had been used to secure the victim were gone. The crime scene had been cleaned up with the same meticulous attention to detail as the other three.

Except, this time, it hadn't – quite.

When the two men had gone to the window to see what was happening outside the killer had touched the rail at the window – and then he'd forgotten about it. Now the rail yielded up its secret to a puff of fine powder and a strip of tape. At last there was a piece of physical evidence, a single fingerprint. The pathologist checked it against Collier's body. It wasn't his, and that meant it could very well belong to the man they were looking for.

The Met now believed they were pursuing a multiple murderer, even if they didn't know the full tally of victims yet. Still, when Collier's murder was reported they didn't mention these suspicions at first. Because of the brutality of the crime it was splashed all over the London and national media, but it wasn't yet publicly linked to any other killings. Over the next few days the CID – Patrick and Finnegan's teams, now under the overall supervision of Detective Chief Superintendent Ken John – slowly built up their picture of the two connected cases, but they kept much of their knowledge to themselves. Finally the publicity-hungry predator's impatience boiled over. On June 12 he closed the door of a call box behind him and picked up the phone.

Detective Constable Gareth Barlow was used to crank calls, so when his phone rang and the man on the other end told him he was a serial killer he was skeptical. That wouldn't last long. When he challenged the caller on why he should be taken seriously the man calmly described how he'd killed a man a few days earlier and left the body with a cat's tail in its mouth. That convinced Barlow this was real. Grabbing his notebook he began scribbling frantically.

Over the next hour three more calls were made, one to each of the stations that had investigated the killings. Each time the caller listed the victims' names and addresses, and asked the police why they hadn't connected them. Now, finally, they did. By the end of June 12 there was no doubt left that all the men had been murdered by a single assailant. As final confirmation Dunn's body was hastily autopsied and faint ligature marks found around his throat. There was a predictable flood of internal recrimination as the Met asked themselves why they hadn't connected the pieces before, but any serious inquiry could wait for later. Right now there was no time to lose – this man had to be found before he killed again.

Then, on June 13, there was another call. It told them they were already too late.

June 12

The Coleherne, London

When Emanuel Spiteri walked into the pub he knew he looked the part. The 41-year-old chef, originally from Malta, loved to dress up in black leather pants and motorcycle boots when he visited The Coleherne. His flamboyant dress was his way of concealing a natural shyness. Short and slender, he usually kept himself to himself and he knew the regulars at the leather bar thought of him as a wallflower, but he enjoyed himself anyway. A few miles away, in the newspaper offices of Wapping and the studios at BBC Television Centre, hundreds of people were working feverishly on the day's big story – that a serial killer was stalking London's gay community. Spiteri knew that a couple of Coleherne regulars had died recently and there were one or two others he hadn't seen in the last couple of weeks, but while he was slightly wary he was blissfully unaware of the true danger. Nevertheless as he sat down with his drink a watchful voice at the back of his mind cautioned him to be careful who he allowed to pick him up. Strangers, once part of the thrill of the leather scene, were now a possible source of danger. He was relieved that the man who approached him was familiar; he'd seen him in here quite a few times before.

The other man – Colin, he said his name was, but who knew how many people here gave their real names? – seemed almost as shy as himself, in a way. They chatted about trivia; soccer, the weather, the war in Bosnia where British troops had just killed two Croat gunmen. Once or twice the conversation touched on the murders of Walker and Collier, and the mysterious death of Dunn – even if the police had been slow to link them many in the gay community had wondered. Colin smiled crookedly. "Worrying, isn't it? Glad there are familiar faces around."

Spiteri nodded. "I know what you mean." He finished his drink then looked down at the table, overcome by shyness. "So... well... want to come back for a while?"

Catford, Southeast London

He'd been too trusting, Spiteri thought bitterly. Of course he'd seen the man before. He'd seen him stalking in his hunting ground. Well, it was probably the last mistake he was ever going to make. He hoped the last minutes weren't going to be too hard, but he was damned if he was going to plead for his life. He twisted his head round to face the man crouched behind the bed. "Well go on, what are you waiting for?"

The man held up Spiteri's bank card. "I want the code for this. Tell me and you'll live."

Spiteri laughed derisively. "Yeah. Like the others? You're going to kill me anyway, so why should I tell you anything?"

"I can make you tell me, you know. I've done it before."

Spiteri believed it, but he planned to hold out as long as he could anyway. Why make things easy for this animal? He held Colin's gaze and shook his head, once, with calm finality. "No."

To his surprise the killer just shrugged. "Alright." He stood up. Suddenly he sounded weary; whatever his reason for doing this, his enthusiasm for it seemed to have gone.

Would that be enough to save him? Spiteri wondered. No, it wouldn't. Perhaps there had been a moment of indecision but now it had passed. Enthusiastically or not, this man was going to kill him. "Do whatever you're going to do," he said.

Colin didn't say anything. He just nodded, picked up a noose from the floor and slipped it over Spiteri's head. Spiteri closed his eyes. A moment later the rope began to tighten.

It was June 15 before Spiteri's body was found, but the police had already been looking for a corpse for two days. On the morning of June 13 the killer had called them to let them know that he'd killed again. He seemed eager to talk; when asked why he was doing this he said he'd read books about serial killers and wanted to see if it was possible to commit a string of killings and get away with it. He'd targeted gays, he explained, because they were reluctant to involve the police – and because he didn't like them. Anyway he'd proven he could do it and probably wouldn't kill again. They weren't likely to hear any more about him, he assured the detective. Finally he suggested they look for a body where there had been a fire.

Two days later a Catford landlady called the local station to say that one of her lodgers was dead. Of natural causes? She didn't think so. There had been a fire in the room, she said, and it didn't look like an accident. A team of detectives was quickly dispatched; they could already guess what they would find, and they were right. Spiteri's body lay on his bed, the marks of the handcuffs, bonds and strangling rope still clear on his discolored skin. His papers and most of the furniture had been heaped in the middle of the floor and set on fire, but the blaze had obviously burned itself out in minutes – little serious damage had been done, and none of the neighbors had even reported smelling smoke. Still, it was obvious that this was the serial killer's fifth victim.

Chapter 9

Early in 1993 Ireland lost his pallet-breaking job. Now he had only his welfare payments to live on – housing benefit to cover his rent, plus £64 – about $98 – in cash every two weeks. He didn't let that interfere with his plans though. He had read many books about serial killers, including *Whoever Fights Monsters* by veteran FBI agent Robert Ressler. From these he identified many of the mistakes that had led to other predators being caught. He was also a fan of TV crime shows and avidly followed the progress of fictional investigations. Long-running ITV series *The Bill* was a rich source of information. The night he killed Dunn he'd had a flashlight in his murder kit. In one episode of the show a criminal had been caught because, while he'd worn gloves during a robbery, he hadn't been wearing them when he loaded the batteries into the flashlight he lost at the scene. Ireland's flashlight had joined the rest of his equipment in a rucksack at the bottom of the canal, but first he'd removed the batteries and slipped them into his pocket for later disposal. "You ought to ban that show," he told the police later.

He planned to target the BDSM scene, so his intended victims should let him tie them up without raising any suspicions, but he couldn't rely on finding suitable restraints in their homes. Rope and handcuffs were added to his kit. He deliberately selected cheap – but functional – cuffs and a common brand of rope, just in case they were found and a memorable purchase led the police to him. He knew that fibers could incriminate him so he carried a spare set of clothes with him and, as he left the crime scenes, changed everything that could have left traces at the scene or carried away evidence that would later place him there. The clothes, shoes and gloves he'd worn to commit each murder would be disposed of with the rest. It was an effective plan, creating an evidential air gap between him and the crimes. After the killings he would wait until morning before leaving the scene because neighbors were more likely to take note of a stranger in the early hours.

In fact he'd planned for everything except the police failing to connect the murders and realize there was a serial killer on the loose. Gaining the notoriety he craved depended on them seeing what was happening and launching a major manhunt – and it didn't happen. It took his phone calls to turn the spotlight on the case.

If there hadn't been enough publicity to suit him after the first three murders, however, now there was plenty. The day Spiteri's body was found the Met held a midnight press conference to announce the fifth death and to warn the gay community that they were all in danger. The timing was carefully calculated; if the killer was watching TV with his next potential victim, the warning might save a life.

The mutual distrust and incomprehension between London's gay men and the Met had been a huge roadblock since Walker's death back in March, but now the cops were determined to bridge it. The Lesbian and Gay Police Association was brought in to present a friendlier face of law enforcement, and at the London Pride festival on June 19 officers were circulating, handing out warning leaflets and imploring people to come forward if they knew anything. Finally it paid off.

One young man who'd seen the press conference and read the leaflet found himself faced with an agonizing decision. His family didn't know he was gay and he feared exposure, but he thought he had information that the police needed. He bit the bullet and called the Met; Albert Patrick would later praise him for having the guts to make such a tough decision. He'd seen Spiteri on a train the night he died, with another man – a big man with a fleshy face and discolored teeth. Unlike many eyewitnesses he was able to give an accurate, detailed description, good enough to start building an image using the new e-fit software that was replacing the old photofit sets. As more witnesses came forward the picture of the suspect was refined, and on June 24 Detective Chief Superintendent Hay was confident enough to release it to the public. They also tracked down the surveillance camera footage from Charing Cross Station, one of the locations Spiteri had been seen, and scanned over 450 hours of tape until they found their target. Spiteri and his companion had been captured by several cameras and at least one of them had delivered the perfect evidence. They now had dozens of clear frames showing Spiteri and a tall, well-built man – and the suspect's face was clearly visible.

On July 2 the police held another press conference, this time aimed directly at the killer. As well as broadcasting an appeal for him to stop killing and talk to them, they released the clearest frame of Spiteri and the other man. Ireland immediately knew he had a problem. He was clearly recognizable in the shot and it could only be a matter of time before somebody – most likely Richard Higgs, who was already uneasy following a conversation with a clearly rattled Ireland hours after Spiteri's death – called the murder hotline with his name. He only had one card left to play, and now he used it. On July 19 he went to his attorney's office in Southend-On-Sea and said he'd like to make a sworn statement.

According to Ireland's account, he'd accepted Spiteri's invitation back to his apartment but backed out at the door. There's been another man already inside, he said, and that had made him nervous. Now, having made the mental connection between that seemingly harmless incident and the murder, he wanted to tell the police what he knew. It was a desperate gambit but it might have worked. The police didn't waste any time checking out the story; they simply told Ireland they'd like to take his fingerprints. It was too late to back out now. The CCTV footage was enough to arrest him on suspicion and then he'd be fingerprinted anyway. In any case, he reasoned, there had been no evidence left at any of the crime scenes. He'd been very careful about that. He agreed to the request and inked his fingers. Andrew Collier's windowsill never crossed his mind.

Two days later Ireland was arrested on suspicion of murder.

Chapter 10

The initial arrest was only for the murder of Collier, but Spiteri's death was added as a second charge on July 23. Ireland denied both killings. He was held on remand, waiting in a police cell while the investigation continued. Outside the station more witnesses came forward, and hints began to emerge that a man similar to Ireland had been seen with other victims on their last visit to The Coleherne. Some gay men, encouraged by the fact that the police were now taking the case as seriously as it deserved, went to their local stations and made statements.

It's impossible to say what was going on inside Ireland's head at this point. He knew that, despite all his precautions, the police now had evidence linking him to at least two of the crimes. His denials might introduce just enough doubt to get him acquitted, but that outcome was far from guaranteed. Anyway on August 19 he dropped his final bombshell. Calling for a guard, he asked to speak to a detective. "I'm the gay serial killer," he said, "Tell the police I want to confess."

Once he'd made the decision to talk, he did so freely. He wanted to change his plea to guilty, he explained. He should be put in a position where he could no longer inflict harm on others. He chatted away about why and how he'd committed the murders, described his victims' last moments in detail, and calmly condemned himself by admitting that he generally disliked people and had an innate capacity for violence. He expressed no remorse for his actions, nor did he brag or gloat – he just gave the facts and his own feelings and impressions. Collier was the only victim he'd been angry at, he said. Spiteri had been a very brave man. Walker, he thought, had subconsciously wanted to die. Had anything bothered him? Yes, he replied. Sitting through the night with the dead men, watching their skin tone change and become blotchy as the blood settled within their bodies had had an effect on him.[xv]

One thing he was very careful to do was to emphasize his complete responsibility for his actions. He hadn't been drunk or on drugs when he'd committed any of the murders. There had been no sexual element and he wasn't gay himself; he'd hunted gay men because they were easy targets, not because of any particular dislike of them (this doesn't fully agree with what Janet Young claimed – she said he hated gays). He told the interviewers that he could just as easily have targeted women. By the time he finished talking the police were utterly convinced that he was a very dangerous man.

As a result of his guilty plea Ireland didn't face a full trial, which would have increased his notoriety. Instead there was just a sentencing hearing on December 20, 1993. It lasted two hours, and the list of aggravating circumstances left even hardened court reporters chilled. His own defense counsel, Andrew Trollope QC, was blunt: There were no mitigating circumstances, he told the court, and no question of diminished responsibility; two psychologists had found his client to be entirely sane. The sentence was already a foregone conclusion. Calling him "an exceptionally frightening and dangerous man" and branding his actions "carnage," judge Sachs sentenced him to life imprisonment and specified that the detention would be "at Her Majesty's pleasure" – an indefinite term. Ireland shrugged. He had already accepted that he would die in prison. As the judgment was read out his mother sobbed in the spectators' gallery. His stepfather, Alan Williams, told the journalists waiting outside the court that the sentence was justified.[xvi] Nobody disagreed.

Conclusion

So what was Colin Ireland? Was he a psychopath? Perhaps; he was manipulative, self-centered and could display a stunning lack of empathy for other people. But many people who knew him well – Virginia Zammit and Richard Higgs, for example – maintain that he had a good side too. It's almost certain that they're right, but if anything that makes his crimes even more horrifying.

Ireland had a tough, dysfunctional childhood and there's no doubt it left him psychologically damaged, but he wasn't beyond salvation. He could, and did, act selflessly and show genuine kindness. His popularity among the residents of the homeless shelter attests to that, and both Zammit's and Janet Young's children adored him. His personality had both good and evil sides and he seems to have been able to choose which one to act on. Faced with that decision he freely chose evil. There was no reason for him to commit the murders he perpetrated. He robbed his victims, but that wasn't the goal – he used the money he stole to buy the equipment and train tickets for the next murder. He killed simply to boost his own status; the decision to become a serial killer was an entirely conscious one and once it was made gay men became nothing more to him than pawns to be expended in reaching his goal. Five men died so Colin Ireland could see his name in the headlines.

Or was it more than five? Albert Patrick believes it was. Ireland was questioned about six more murders as well as the five he finally confessed to. The retired detective strongly suspects that Ireland was responsible for at least one of them. In January 1993 a gay man was tied up and killed in his apartment. His body wasn't found for several days and in that time his two pet dogs, driven by starvation, had eaten most of it. Patrick thinks that the grisly details of that death were too much even for Ireland and that he denied responsibility out of either queasiness or embarrassment. It's striking that in the only other case where the victim had dogs – Peter Walker – Ireland locked them in another room. Was it to keep them out of the way while he worked, or to keep them away from the body?

We'll never know the answer now, because Colin Ireland is fortunately no longer with us. On February 11, 2012 he fell in the exercise yard of Wakefield Prison and broke his hip, leaving him unable to get around without a Zimmer frame or wheelchair. Ten days later he was found dead on the floor of his cell. The autopsy results showed that he'd died from a combination of the fractured pelvis and pulmonary fibrosis.[xvii] It was a much less dramatic, more merciful and less capricious death than the ones he'd inflicted on at least five men and a cat. We're all looking for justice in life but it's pretty hard to see it sometimes.

[i] People, Jul 12, 1993; *A Killer Stalks Gay London*

http://www.people.com/people/archive/article/0,,20110794,00.html

[ii] Channel 5, Aug 21, 2012; *Born To Kill? – The Gay Slayer*
http://www.channel5.com/shows/born-to-kill/episodes/the-gay-slayer

[iii] The Independent, Dec 21, 1993; *Serial killer locked up for life*
http://www.independent.co.uk/news/serial-killer-locked-up-for-life-to-take-one-human-life-is-an-outrage-to-take-five-is-carnage-says-judge-1468716.html

[iv] The Independent, Dec 21, 1993; *Serial killer locked up for life*
http://www.independent.co.uk/news/serial-killer-locked-up-for-life-to-take-one-human-life-is-an-outrage-to-take-five-is-carnage-says-judge-1468716.html

[v] BBC Radio 1 interview transcript, *The Enid*
http://www.designdetector.com/interviews/the-enid-interviewed-by-tommy-vance.html

[vi] CrimeLibrary, *Colin Ireland*

http://www.crimelibrary.com/serial_killers/predators/ireland/page_6.html

[vii] Samaritans, *How Samaritans Started*
http://www.samaritans.org/about-us/history-samaritans

[viii] Channel 5, Aug 21, 2012; *Born To Kill? – The Gay Slayer*
http://www.channel5.com/shows/born-to-kill/episodes/the-gay-slayer

[ix] CrimeLibrary, *Colin Ireland*

http://www.crimelibrary.com/serial_killers/predators/ireland/page_6.html
[x] CrimeLibrary, *Colin Ireland*

http://www.crimelibrary.com/serial_killers/predators/ireland/page_7.html
[xi] Channel 5, Aug 21, 2012; *Born To Kill? – The Gay Slayer*
http://www.channel5.com/shows/born-to-kill/episodes/the-gay-slayer
[xii] Crime & Investigation, *Colin Ireland*
http://crimeandinvestigation.co.uk/crime-files/colin-ireland/serial-criminal
[xiii] People, Jul 12, 1993; *A Killer Stalks Gay London*

http://www.people.com/people/archive/article/0,,20110794,00.html
[xiv] Channel 5, Aug 21, 2012; *Born To Kill? – The Gay Slayer*
http://www.channel5.com/shows/born-to-kill/episodes/the-gay-slayer
[xv] Channel 5, Aug 21, 2012; *Born To Kill? – The Gay Slayer*
http://www.channel5.com/shows/born-to-kill/episodes/the-gay-slayer
[xvi] The Independent, Dec 21, 1993; *Serial killer locked up for life*
http://www.independent.co.uk/news/serial-killer-locked-up-for-life-to-take-one-human-life-is-an-outrage-to-take-five-is-carnage-says-judge-1468716.html
[xvii] Pink News, Feb 292, 2012; *Exercise yard fall contributed to death of 'Gay Slayer', inquest hears*
http://www.pinknews.co.uk/2012/02/29/exercise-yard-fall-contributed-to-death-of-gay-slayer-inquest-hears/

Printed in Great Britain
by Amazon